# GUY TALK

## COLLEGE SENIORS' ADVICE FOR INCOMING FRESHMEN

Written by Andrew J. Sotis

This book is intended for educational and entertainment purposes only. At no point is illegal activity encouraged or the commission of crime condoned. In no way, shape, or form is this book affiliated with the University of St. Thomas.

If you find yourself feeling offended at any point while reading, please follow the steps below:

1.   Stop reading the book.

ISBN: 1545164053

ISBN-13: 9781545164051

# INTRODUCTION

## PLEASE READ!

Recent and soon-to-be high school graduates, this book is my attempt to help out the next generation of college students—a college advice guide *for* guys *from* guys.

You might be asking, "Who do you think you are? Why would anyone read your shit?"

Fair questions. Who cares about some guy with an opinion? He's probably some kid whose mom told him he could do anything he put his mind to. Maybe he just wanted to write a book in the hopes of becoming more like Hank Moody. (Look him up.)

You're right—anyone can publish anything these days. Free speech is dope.

To answer your questions, this is not only my personal account. More than thirty of my roommates, friends, professors, and family members (listed in the Acknowledgements section) helped by brainstorming, sharing their stories, and editing this book. Just know that most of the material is coming not from one random dude but from a plethora of different perspectives. Yes, this advice came from a relatively slimmer sample size, considering many of us attended the same midsize private school in the Midwest, but many of these tips, tricks, and stories apply universally to residential colleges nationwide. Regardless of whether you go to a massive state school or a tiny Bible college, this book has something for you.

Still, I do think it's important to establish some level of personal credibility so that, in your eyes, I'm more than just some twenty-two-year-old typing away on his laptop. Time for a little background. To you or me, the following "accomplishments" may not mean much, but they could make a difference to your parents or relatives, who might be buying this book for you.

On paper, I've had a successful college experience:

- I chilled with the nerd herd in student government as senior class president.

- I served as captain of my lacrosse team in my junior and senior years.

- I landed an engineering internship right out of high school, where I worked for two summers.

- For the two summers afterwards, I had the incredible opportunity to live in Guatemala and work with a missions organization.

- I graduated with a bachelor's degree in mechanical engineering in May 2017 and had my dream job lined up eight months prior to receiving my diploma.

I am by no means trying to boast, but maybe now some of you looking to be "successful" during and after college have decided that I might have some words of wisdom for you.

There are countless things my friends and I wish we had known freshman year. This book is our best attempt at writing those down. We want you to kill it in school, have tons of fun, save money for you and your family, and land poised for a bright future.

Much of what you've heard about college is wrong. For several reasons that I'll explain later on, we want you to get past the classic "college student" mentality. More goes on at school than drinking all day and hooking up with as many girls as you can.

This is not a moral handbook, and I am not your mother, but your behavior and decision-making during college have the potential to radically change your future, and we would suggest using this advice to your advantage.

We don't expect you to follow every piece of advice we offer. Some of it may not apply to your school's social or academic environment. Still, we are confident that there's enough here for you to sink your teeth into.

**This book is far from perfect. I am not a writer. Maybe you'll read a sentence that seems poorly written. Maybe you feel offended because something I say isn't politically correct. Maybe you notice design or organizational flaws. Good! Let it be a reminder that this book was written by people like you, ballin' on a budget, just four years ahead. It's meant to be real. And helpful. Not perfect.**

I hope you enjoy reading our thoughts and reaping the benefits. Good luck, you college-bound man, you.

To Dad

# ACKNOWLEDGMENTS

\*\*\*\*\*\*\*\*\*\* Illustrated by Tanner Ahlborn \*\*\*\*\*\*\*\*\*\*

A huge thank you to everyone who made this happen. Brainstormers, interviewees, peer editors…they did it all:

Geoff McQuillan

David Kalish

Michael Cossette

Kameren Lymon

Matthew Cutshall

Laini Schneider

Will Pavek

Cody Kaye

Jessie O'Brien

Lauren Keller

Brittney Krebsbach

Darcy Dean

Nicholas Bruno

Matthew Meshbesher

Andrew Broman

Simon Gondeck

J. B. Stender

Jackie Ellingson

Robbie Ellingson

Paige Healy

Evan Nolander

Patrick Kegley

Sara Sargent

Dr. Nelson-Cheeseman

Graham Provencher

Kellie & Kimberly from CreateSpace

Jody Zipp

**VIPs:**

Maia Sotis

Lisa Sotis

Bill Sotis

# CONTENTS

# CHAPTER 1: PREGAME

STUFF TO KNOW/DO BEFORE HEADING TO SCHOOL

## 1.1 FINDING A ROOMMATE

The roommate situation can be a large factor in your overall freshman experience. Your decisions and mentality in the process of finding and living with someone may lead to a new best friend or a constant thorn in your side. This person is going to be with you every day, whether you speak or not, for the first year of your life at school.

Take some time to think about what you want in a roommate.

- Are you a morning person?

- Do you plan to be a party animal or keep it low key?

- Are women's studies a priority, or do you like hanging with the guys?

- Do you mind if he's messy? Be honest.

- Do you care if he stumbles in at 3:00 a.m.?

- If he has a girlfriend, will it bug you if she's over all the time?

- What kind of relationship would you like to have with him? Partner in crime? Or simple coexistence?

## PRO TIPS

It's tempting to live with a high school friend. We say don't do it. Sure, you were best buddies senior year, but living together can change that. College is a completely different environment from high school, and many of these yearbook friendships don't prosper as much as people anticipate. But choosing the safe route by picking someone familiar is something we advise against for a bigger reason. We want you to be open to the unknown, to different people with different experiences and perspectives. A main theme of this book is branching out—discovering new things and people—and rooming with your best buddy from high school can encourage complacency with the friendship you have instead of motivating you to go out and meet all types of new people.

Facebook groups for incoming freshmen are a great place to find a roommate. Your school should have a group set up for the incoming class by the spring semester before you start school, and you should definitely take advantage of it. There you can also check out the gorgeous gals you'll be getting to know.

Roomsurf.com is another good resource. When finding a roommate using a network like this one, you and others can post short bios about who you are, where you hail from, what you like to do, and what kind of lifestyle you're looking to live at school. Contact others if they seem like they might be a good match. Ask questions that might reveal potential deal-breakers for you.

### FINAL THOUGHTS

Choose someone new who seems cool enough for you. Afterward, it is your job to make the most of the relationship.

(See 2.7 "Roommate Relations.")

# 1.2 DORM SELECTION

*Not all dorms are created equal.*

*–Dave Kalish*

Living in a freshman dorm is probably one of the most unique living experiences you'll ever have. Don't commute during your freshman year. If money is a huge issue, do what you gotta do to live in a dorm, and then commute from home in the years afterward if you need to save money. (By then, the majority of your relationships will have taken root.)

Dorm reputations spread like gossip, and these reputations influence the types of people who apply to live in them, further enforcing their reputations. Your job is to find out the rep of every dorm on your campus ahead of time. Search online or ask anyone you might know at the school already for the inside scoop on what each dorm is like.

Do your research and find out what each dorm has to offer.

Try to answer these questions when evaluating your options.

- Does it have a dining hall? Study rooms? Printers?

- What's the vibe of the people who tend to live there? Quiet? Party animals?

- Are the resident advisers (RAs) known to be strict or lenient? (See section 2.8.)

- Is it an all-guys dorm or a mixed dorm? Girls in every other room? Separated by floor?

- Is it in a safe area or a sketchy part of town? How long is the walk to your classes?

- How close is it to other dorms? Is it isolated?

## PRO TIPS

The *quality* of your dorm room's living space does not matter. Don't pick a dorm with a lousy reputation because the furniture is new and you have private bathrooms. Screw that.

Go with a social dorm over a quiet, mellow one. If you're outgoing and love to make friends, definitely live in a social atmosphere. If you're more introverted and struggle with new relationships, still, live in a social atmosphere. Freshman year is when everyone is open to making new friends, so take advantage of it. You have the rest of your life to watch Netflix alone in your own quiet, boring apartment. Don't pass up the opportunity to meet some awesome people and potentially lifelong friends because you're scared of missing a few hours of sleep from the noise. It's one year—get out of your comfort zone. If you do not end up living in  a social dorm, befriend guys who do.

The relationships you create as a freshman are the foundation for the rest of your years at school. Even if you have only a few conversations with the other people living in your dorm, you'll be saying "what's up?" to one another on campus until you graduate. Even if you don't end up staying friends with the guys from your dorm, there's a good chance you will meet your new friends through them.

Location isn't everything. True, if your dorm room is a forty-minute walk from your lecture, it's going to be easy to let yourself skip; however, we still think social reputation trumps location.

## • STORY TIME •

Our dorms were all guys. It was amazing. You could walk around naked and pee in the sinks. The idea of having girls living right next door to you sounds awesome, but living on a floor with fifty of your homies is pretty sick too. Keep in mind most guys are cooler when their lady friends are not around.

## FINAL THOUGHTS

Pick a dorm that's known to be social. Losing a few hours of sleep to noisy neighbors will be worth it.

# 1.3 DORM ROOM PREPARATION

Dorm life is great. Bringing the right stuff can make it even better. Here are a few categories of things you might want to consider bringing to the great outdorms to have an awesome time after leaving the nest. Make sure you coordinate with your roommate(s) before buying anything; you don't want to waste money on stuff they may already have or end up with three mini fridges you need to stack to the ceiling.

This is not a complete packing list - just some things we'd recommend thinking about bringing to school. We've excluded obvious items (e.g., clothes and a toothbrush).

## HOMINESS
Mattress pad, extra blankets, floor rug

## FOOD STUFF
Keurig coffeemaker or coffeepot, microwave, thermos or travel mug, Tupperware, pizza maker, paper plates, plastic ware, microwave-safe plastic bowls, coffee mug, water bottle, mini fridge

## ELECTRONICS
Long charging cords, power strip, extension cords, fan, HDMI cord, small lamp, speaker of some sort, book light, Christmas lights

## CLEANLINESS
Paper towels, Tide to Go, lint brush, Clorox wipes, trash bags, small trash bin, Ziploc bags, laundry detergent, dryer sheets, Febreze

## STORAGE
Shoe rack, tiered clothes hanger, laundry basket, 3M wall hooks, small plastic bins

## HYGIENE/HEALTH
Shower caddy that can get wet, shower shoes (narsty shtuff in the showers), underbed storage, first-aid kit, Emergen-C, Kleenex, cough/cold meds

## OTHER
Sports equipment (intramurals), toolbox (including hammer, nails, duct tape, screwdriver, and scissors), lockbox, earplugs

## PRO TIPS

Communicate with your roommate(s) early on. Make a plan and agree on who's bringing what.

Once you move in, make a spare key at a local hardware store. Schools often make you pay a fat replacement fee for lost keys.

Don't cause permanent damage in your room.

Loft your beds if possible. (If you don't know what this means, picture your mattress on five-foot stilts.)This will help maximize your minimal floor space.

Do not buy a printer. The cost of ink is ridiculous. Use the printers on campus. Most likely, you'll have a printing allowance or pay a very small fee, which is a lot less inexpensive that buying your own ink would be.

One of your most important investments when coming to college may be a good pair of headphones. Spending a few extra dollars here is worth it.

# 1.4 CLASS REGISTRATION & SCHEDULE

Decisions in the registration process really affect your life at school.

Getting shafted with bad professors or a rough class schedule can make a semester tough to get through. You don't want to find yourself wasting hours on pointless busywork or not learning anything at all. I'm guessing you'd like a course schedule that both fits your desired lifestyle and helps motivate you to learn.

When preparing for registration, ask yourself:

- Do you know what field you'd like to major in, or are you solidly undecided?

- Are you a morning person? Will you get up for an 8:00 a.m. lecture?

- How do you learn best? From listening to lectures? Studying on your own?

- If attendance isn't mandatory, will you still go to class?

## ACTION ITEMS

- Put in the work to plan your schedule before registration. This can save you a lot of precious time once registration begins, when classes fill up quickly.

- Find the best-rated professors for each requirement you need to fulfill.

- Make a four-year plan with an academic adviser at your school. Advisers know what's going on and what is realistic. If you can't sit down with yours, e-mail your plan to him or her and ask for feedback.

- Have a backup plan. Typically, students closer to graduation get to register first. Since you're a freshman, many classes you're interested in will be full by the time you register. Have two or three good options for each course in case your initial choices are taken.

- If a class you're interested in is full, send an e-mail to the professor asking nicely if he or she can let you in. Explain why it's important. Your professors may have the authority to override the registration capacity for one or two extra students. Otherwise, you may have to reach out to the department chair.

## PRO TIPS

If you're not a morning person, don't kid yourself. It's nice to imagine yourself waking up for an 8:00 a.m. lecture and getting your day started, but if that's going to be a struggle, don't set yourself up for failure.

Professors matter. A lot. More than the course topic or description. Get that through your head. **One of your best friends in college should be ratemyprofessors.com.** Students write descriptions of professors' tendencies; demands; difficulty levels; and most importantly, hotness. Taking one hour to research professors and their reputations before registration can save you many hours of studying.

A forced-attendance policy can be helpful to make sure you stay on top of things, but sometimes a more flexible professor is beneficial. Some days you might have to skip class to finish an essay or project. And depending on how you learn, it might be a better use of your time to teach yourself the material rather than sitting through lectures without retaining anything.

Make sure the classes you are taking will satisfy a graduation requirement. You don't want to find out that you wasted your time and money on something that did not help you toward graduating.

During your first semester, take only one class in your major field if you think you know what you want to study. If you take a full major load, you may be wasting a ton of time and money if you end up switching majors.

Balance your course load over multiple semesters. You probably don't want to take only easy general courses freshman year. Space out the more difficult classes (most likely within your major field) across your four years—don't save them all until the end.

### FINAL THOUGHTS

Save time and money by planning your academic schedule throughout your four years. Don't set yourself up for failure with problem professors or bad lecture times.

## 1.5 CHOOSE A MEAL PLAN

Living on campus is usually coupled with buying a meal plan for each semester. First-semester students (and their parents) often waste a ton of money by buying too large a meal plan. Choosing the right plan can save you and your family a decent chunk of money.

So how do you choose? This depends on your lifestyle and what your school has to offer. Ask yourself:

- Are you an athlete with two workouts a day or a 110-pound computer geek?

- Do you plan to eat most of your meals in dining halls, or will employees at all the nearby fast-food restaurants know your name?

- What will your class schedule look like? Does it allow you time to eat breakfast?

An à la carte–style meal plan works like buying food from a grocery store or gas station: the school charges you for each item individually. In this case, find out if it'll be cheaper to buy from your school or elsewhere. On-campus convenience stores are usually overpriced because they are—you guessed it—convenient. Even if your school's options are more expensive, you might be stuck with the higher prices if there are limited options for food within walking distance.

Many schools offer an all-you-can-eat or buffet-style meal plan, where the cost is determined by the number of meal swipes you're allowed in dining halls for a given semester. Make sure your class schedule will allow you to eat when you want to. Depending on your school, you may not be able to use a meal swipe for dinner after seven or eight o'clock.

## OUR ADVICE:

- Do the math. Compare the cost of meals vs. buying food out vs. grocery shopping. Make a plan based on your anticipated eating habits. Keep in mind the amount of time saved when you don't have to cook and clean up after yourself.

- You will not eat three meals at an all-you-can-eat dining hall every day. The biggest plan usually provides you with enough meals to accomplish this feat. Don't buy it. You won't use all of your meal swipes. On top of that, you'll get sick of eating the same food every day long before the end of the semester.

- Buying groceries and carrying food with you (instead of buying snacks from campus convenience stores) can save you a lot of money.

- Smuggle fruit and snacks out of the dining hall.

- We'd recommend one or two all-you-can-eat meals a day freshman year. Even one of these meals can make a huge difference in time saved and money spent on food throughout the rest of the day.

- Get into a good habit of trying new foods, eating healthy, and avoiding the temptation to eat pizza and a burger every day first semester.

## FINAL THOUGHTS

*Live by the meal plan, imma die by the meal plan.*

*-Waka Flocka Flame*

# 1.6 TEXTBOOKS ARE SATAN

If you're into lighting bundles of twenty-dollar bills on fire, shop at your campus bookstore.

Making bad decisions when buying textbooks can waste five grand over the course of your four years. That's $3.42 poorly spent every day. That's one tall pumpkin spice latte for your basic girlfriend every single morning.

## EXCEPTION:

The only time you might be forced to buy a brand-new textbook is if it comes with an online homework or testing component that requires a single-use activation code. Try looking online for a cheaper brand-new book that comes with an unused code before resorting to your school's bookstore.

## PRO TIPS

Don't buy your books before your classes start. Many schools require professors to list a textbook for their courses, and they don't always end up using it. Wait to see if you absolutely need to get one. (You'll have a feel for this after the first few lectures.) If your professor assigns a reading to be discussed the first day of class, he or she sucks.

*Do not buy from your school's bookstore.* A brand-new, pretty-looking textbook doesn't make you smarter. Wasting $300 is also not an indication of intelligence. Bookstores try to convince you that new books are a smart investment because they'll buy your books back at the end of the semester. Most likely, you'll get twenty bucks back on your $300 "investment." Also, don't be afraid to make friends with older students in your classes. They can be a great resource for cheap used books in the future. If you do end up buying a hard copy of your textbook and want to sell it at the end of the semester, check out options other than your bookstore. Selling to your peers, to Amazon, or bookscouter.com may be the smarter move.

Search online for a free PDF download of the desired book. Many textbooks are available for use and/or download online for free.

Split the cost and share with someone in class, preferably a girl. Girls are smart and usually have their shit together when it comes to classes. (We have a lot to learn from them.) Become study buddies. Or spouses.

Rent your books online if doing so is cheaper than buying. Amazon usually has pretty fair prices for renting a book on a semester basis. Don't be all "I think I'd like to keep my textbook so I can reference it in the future." You're not a professor. Chances are you won't. Google is a thing.

You don't have to buy the newest edition of most textbooks. No, there probably are not groundbreaking new discoveries in the new edition. They changed some fonts, colors, and page numbers as an excuse to republish the book and make more money off you. If you have to buy, go with an older edition and save cash. Check out Amazon, AbeBooks, ValoreBooks, and other online booksellers.

# 1.7 SCHOLARSHIPS

Landing a few scholarships outside of your school's initial financial-aid offer can save you stacks on stacks. This is another area you really should put some time into researching the summer before going to school—and every summer afterward.

Your school most likely offers a wide variety of scholarships to its students. There are countless scholarships offered independently of your university as well. You might be eligible for a ridiculous number of random scholarships. Your job is to find them and apply.

## • STORY TIME •

My roommate won a $5,000 scholarship just for being Polish; Catholic; and from Duluth, Minnesota. Find your niche. Be willing to write an essay, and you might get some cash.

## PRO TIPS

Look deep into your family tree and prove that you're not 100 percent white.

If you know what major you'd like to study, go to that specific school's website to see if it offers scholarship competitions.

Look into service-, hometown-, leadership-, or innovation-based awards you may be eligible for.

Apply, apply, apply for any scholarship you may qualify for. One hour could save you and your family $1,000.

## SCHOLARSHIP ORGANIZATIONS TO CHECK OUT:

Scholarships.com, Fastweb, Peterson's, Unigo, Cappex, the College Board, and Niche.

# CHAPTER 2:
# GETTING STARTED

IT IS IN YOUR BEST INTEREST TO START OFF STRONG

## 2.1 WELCOME WEEK

Welcome week is unreal. You've left the nest. First taste of freedom. No one to report to…no curfew. You've been counting down the days, and finally moving in is exciting as hell. Everyone is in the same boat; everyone is in a new environment. Remember that. Welcome week is the time to be a "yes-man"—say yes to any plans that come up.

Looking back, this initial period was very important. First semester of freshman year may be one of the only times in your life when everyone looks forward to meeting you. Keep that in mind whenever you're around new people. Especially for the first few weeks of college, all doors are open, and you want to stick your foot in all of them before they start to close.

Now's the time to man up. Even if you're not normally confident, you should try to force yourself to be. Everyone wants to make friends just as much as you do. Most will be relieved when you introduce yourself— they probably were trying to muster up the balls to do the same. **The best advice I received the summer before leaving for college was from my dad's college roommate: in the first month of school, go up to every single girl you run into and introduce yourself.**

## • STORY TIME •

During welcome week of our freshman year, our school hosted a headphone disco. This meant that everyone was dancing at a silent rave with headphones on. Shit was hilarious - one of the most fun nights of college. I stained and ruined a pair of shorts from dancing with a girl who was wearing brand-new jeans. A lot of people didn't go because it sounded lame, and they completely missed out on the party. Don't be too cool to have fun.

## PRO TIPS

Hold out your hand and confidently introduce yourself to everyone. Network, network, network. As you'll find out a few semesters down the road, the window of time in which people in your class are all extremely friendly and excited to meet you will close, so take advantage of it right away.

Have some go-to small talk ready if you're not quick on your feet. Always ask questions: Where are you from? What dorm are you living in? What do you want to study? Why'd you want to come to school here? People love to talk about themselves, so give them a chance. It doesn't take much to get a conversation started.

Do not wear your lanyard around your neck or let it hang out of your pocket like a sixteen-year-old who wants everyone to know that he drove himself to school.

If there are events planned during Welcome Week, go to them. Even if they sound lame. Even if you feel awkward. You are not too cool for anything. Sometimes there's free food. Get excited to meet your fellow classmates and the friends you'll have for the next four-plus years. Get there and get something out of it.

Make a *huge* effort to remember names. Use other people's names multiple times in your first conversation, and chances are they'll stick.

People will hear stories about you and your behavior. Reputations last, especially at a smaller school. Don't ruin your reputation in the first few nights of college. As *Superbad* put it, "people don't forget."

## FINAL THOUGHTS

Force yourself to be uncomfortable. Spread those wings and fly.

# 2.2 MAKE FRIENDS

Again, your first semester at school is the best time to meet as many people as possible. Be a social butterfly early on, when it's easy. I met most of my friends, later roommates, and future groomsmen during my first few weeks of college.

Friend networks grow exponentially when school gets rollin'. Lay as many foundations as you can early on. Even if a person looks like someone you wouldn't affiliate with, don't judge a book by its cover. Never say no to a first invitation. Even if your initial friends don't end up your BFFs, you most likely will find your long-term friends through their networks.

That being said, it is A-OK to choose *not* to hang out with certain people after you get to know them. College is different from high school: now you have the freedom to *choose* your friends. Open yourself up to the awesome people and opportunities around you, but don't compromise your values to fit in.

## PRO TIPS

So...what are some ways to get out and meet people first semester?

Leave your dorm room door open, and invite your floor mates over whenever possible. Nothing better than chillin' with the boys and meeting some new ones. One thing can lead to another, and one of you may hear of a party or get invited to something. Then, before you know it, the whole squad ends up on an adventure. Get to know the guys around you. Inviting yourself to something or asking to tag along with a friend to something is not a bad thing at this point.

Join clubs, intramurals, Greek life, or sports teams. Schools offer so many cool clubs and events; take advantage. Just stop into a club meeting and test out the waters. If you don't like it, don't go back. Get out there and see what and who your new school has to offer. Intramural sports are a blast and a great opportunity to hang out with people. Next thing you know, you're gettin' beers with the other team after the game.

We strongly suggest meeting as many women as possible. Hang out in the girls' dorms. They're just as excited to meet and hang out with you as you are to meet and hang out with them. You want women on your side—if you're interested in someone a few years down the road, she'll be asking her friends about you and whether you're a good guy. Also, good-looking girls get invited to everything, which isn't always the case for freshmen guys. Tag along, and they might be your ticket.

## FINAL THOUGHTS

Again…Put yourself out there!

## 2.3 NEW YOU

College is a fresh start. Forget the high school reputation. Didn't like who you were or who you hung out with in high school? Now you have a perfect opportunity to change. Maybe you were a douche in high school and you want to be a nice person. Maybe you were a huge pothead and want to lay off the loud. What do you want to work on, now that you've been given this great gift of a clean slate?

- What did you like about your high school self?
- Which past attitudes or behaviors are you not too proud of?
- How would you like to change now that you're in college?

## FINAL THOUGHTS

Use the fresh start to your benefit. Change for the better.

# 2.4 INDEPENDENCE & PEER PRESSURE

In high school, social pressures often encourage you to conform. This is not the case in college. Now's the time to have a backbone and stand behind who you are and what you do. People will think it's cool if you do your own thing and have your own interests and beliefs. If they don't think that's cool, congrats—you've found exactly who you do *not* want to be friends with.

"No thanks, homie."

Whether it's with drinking, drugs, women, or anything else, if you truly don't want to do something, *don't do it.* Yes, we want you to try things out and be more of a yes-man, but this has its limits. Stand by your convictions, and your friends will respect you for it. You don't need an excuse to say no.

## • STORY TIME •

One of the coolest dudes I knew was on my lacrosse team. Let's call him Steve. Steve never touched a drop of alcohol or thought about doing drugs. He was the most disciplined person I knew. He studied, worked out, and focused on reaching his goal of working for the FBI. Steve was supercool and respected by our whole team (which, as a whole, liked to party). He still hung out with the guys over the weekend and had a good time. If you want to be like Steve, be like Steve.

## 2.5 STICK AROUND

*Just hold on we're goin' home. –Drizzy*

For the first few months at school, I recommend against Drake's well-known advice on going home, even if you live close by. Again, the optimal time window for meeting people will end, so the initial time at school is very important. You don't want to get into the habit of wasting your weekends sitting on your parents' couch. Opportunity cost.

Your school is your new home—and most likely will be for four years. Acclimate yourself. Check out parks, restaurants, or concert venues. Uber is always there for you, so not having wheels is not an excuse. Make the most of what your new environment has to offer; you'll be there for a while.

At the same time, expect that you will have moments (or days) when you miss home and family and wonder if you can stick it out. Do what you gotta do to be mentally healthy when you're feeling homesick, but stay on campus. FaceTime your family or high school friends. Make plans to have your parents or friends visit you on a weekend. By second semester, homesickness generally starts to taper off.

## PRO TIPS

Try not to go home until Thanksgiving break. By this time, you'll have established a lot of friendships.

Explore your new environment. If you don't have a car, try to buy a cheap bike on Craigslist. And a lock.

A phone call to your momz can help with homesickness. She'll appreciate it too.

# 2.6 YEARBOOK FRIENDS

Your school is your new home, and you should try to live in the present, fully engaged in your new environment, as much as possible. That being said, we don't want you to burn bridges with your old friends.

## • STORY TIME •

I learned this the hard way from one of my best friends from high school. Fred was interested in remaining best friends, while I was totally focused on my newfound friends and life on campus. It hurt Fred's feelings when I stopped keeping in touch with him. I see Fred every so often, but I don't know if I'll ever be good friends with him again. My actions told him that he wasn't important to me. Don't make the same mistake I did.

## PRO TIPS

Keep in touch with the people you care about from home; they're the ones who got you where you are. This applies to family, teachers, and coaches as well. Don't completely cut off your past relationships the day you move in. All it takes is a text or call every once in a while.

Go visit your friends' schools if you can. You'll understand their lives and have an awesome time seeing their campuses and meeting their friends. When you're at your high school buddy's wedding in the future, it will be nice to know his college friends already.

When your high school friends all go to the same school as you, things can get tricky. Don't limit yourself to hanging out with only them. There are so many cool new people for you to get to know out there. Again, hanging out with only the people who know you from high school may keep you from developing into the kind of person you want to be. They expect you to act and be a certain way, and your changing might come with some turbulence.

### FINAL THOUGHTS

Don't be afraid if you lose some of your friends. It'll happen. Separation is natural. Put in 80 percent effort for new friends and 20 percent for old.

I hate to contradict yet another famous poet, but "no new friends" does not apply here. Sorry Drizzy.

# 2.7 ROOMMATE RELATIONS

No matter whether your roommate is your new best friend or a quiet acquaintance, it's nice to coexist peacefully in your new little box of a home. Start your relationship off on the right note by establishing some expectations for the year, and most likely your roommate experience will go swimmingly. Just as in any relationship, communication is key. Some people are very sensitive to a roommate's behavior.

You may have covered some of these topics when initially finding your roommate. If you have not had these conversations, you need to do so. Ask your roomie:

- What is his intended sleep schedule? What does he need it to be?
- What are his pet peeves when it comes to his living space?
- Which of his things are OK for you to use?

## • STORY TIME •

I lived in a triple my freshman year, and I was not the best roommate. The three of us got along great. I loved sharing the few things I had to offer with my two roommates and always assumed they felt the same way with their things. I depended on using and borrowing their things too often, until it was a habit for me to use things without asking. It worked out, and we're still good friends today, but I'd strongly suggest trying to be more self-sufficient than I was.

## PRO TIPS

If you have a bad first few weeks, don't throw in the towel. Make moves to better your relationship. Communicate through your problems and move forward.

Don't do everything together. Even if you end up best friends, you don't want to make it a necessity to invite/include your roommate in everything you do. This might lead to his getting upset when one day he's not invited to something.

Respect your roommate's personal space and possessions. Ask

before using his stuff. Don't get into the habit of assuming what's his is yours, even if you feel that way about sharing your stuff.

Be honest. If you have booze or drugs in the room and your roommate wouldn't be cool with it, he has the right to know—it's his room too. Just let him know that if anything happens, you'll take the blame; don't hide it from him.

If something he does is a pet peeve of yours, he probably doesn't know it. Let him know what's bugging you. Express your concern right away. If you let those annoyances add up, before you know it, two months later you'll snap in his face. No fun.

If it's been a toxic atmosphere for a while (at least give it a few months), maybe it's time to change it up. Talk to your RA or dorm supervisor to see if it's possible to find a new roommate at the end of the semester.

Keep in mind that your roommate has just as much say in decisions as you do. Don't expect him to behave just as you'd like him to. If he's grinding your gears, find a way to be cool with it.

### • STORY TIME •

One of my best friends freshman year did not get along with her three other roommates at all. To make the most of the situation, she crashed on her other friends' couches some nights and tried not to let it bother her. It was still "the best year of [her] life." Even if it's not an optimal situation, don't let your relationship with your roommate determine the fun and success of your freshman experience.

### FINAL THOUGHTS

Be less sensitive and more open-minded when living with a new roommate. Make it a habit to act in a way that shows respect for his life and living space.

# 2.8 RAs & DORM SAFETY

Your relationship with your floor's resident adviser is important. He can get you and your friends in trouble or save your asses. Please acknowledge this power.

Most RAs take the job either because they enjoy helping people out, being a virgin, feeling powerful, or saving money on rent. You should be able to tell which within the first five minutes of meeting him/her.

## PRO TIPS

RAs put up with a bunch of BS every day. Don't add to it. Chances are they don't really want to write you up for anything—most likely they'll have annoying paperwork to do if they get you in trouble, so don't give them a strong enough reason to.

Cooperate; be honest and respectful. Being a dick will help you 0% of the time.

Some RAs are psychos who hate their jobs and hate you. In this case, just stay out of their way. Don't cause any trouble, and especially don't give them reasons to hate you more.

When it comes to booze/drugs, the less the RA sees, the better, even if you think he's cool with it. If you have people over and hear a knock on the door, open it just enough to talk to him, but don't let him see inside. Somewhat like police, if an RA physically sees a cause for concern, he might be obligated to do something about it. Even if he knows you're drinking, don't let him see inside your room when he's at the door; that way, there's a better chance he'll let you be.

## FINAL THOUGHTS

Respect 'em, and they'll respect you.

# 2.9 LAUNDRY

(It's not that hard.)

If you've never done your own laundry until now (I hadn't), the time has come. Laundry isn't complicated, but you can ruin your clothes if you mess it up. If done incorrectly, the simple art of washing your clothes may take you multiple days and too many trips to the laundry room.

Doing laundry right means not only cleaning your clothes, but also making them last and saving time in the process. Here are some tips to help you become a laundry-room champion.

## • STORY TIME •

To save money and do fewer loads, I got away with separating my clothes into only two loads during my four years. I washed athletic (dri-FIT) clothes on cold and the rest on warm. I didn't ruin much, though a few white T-shirts got dingy over time.

## PRO TIPS

When in doubt, ask your lady friends for advice.

### WASHING

When in doubt, wash on cold. This makes it less likely that clothes will fade, bleed, or shrink. Separate your clothes into three different loads for optimal washing: darks, lights, and delicates (athletic clothing/anything you deem as delicate). Wash darks on cold, lights on warm or hot if they're really dirty but cold otherwise, and delicates on cold.

### DRYING

Always dry on low heat. This causes less shrinkage and general wear and tear on your fabrics. Fold your clothes right away when they finish drying. If they sit in the dryer for two hours after the fact, they'll be wrinkly as balls. Use dryer sheets. If you forget to, your athletic clothes will be staticky, and your nipples will look like diamonds.

## SCHEDULE

Do not do your laundry on Sunday nights. Sundays are the days when most people realize they have to get their shit together, and doing their laundry makes them feel productive. All the washers and dryers will be taken, and the process could take six hours. Pick one time a week when you plan on doing your laundry (midnight on Tuesdays or Thursday mornings, for example). Stick to the plan, and the laundry process will not be a pain; instead, it'll run like a well-oiled machine. Force yourself to finish an assignment during a wash cycle. Call your family or catch up on your reading while she's a-dryin'. Use the fixed time to your advantage.

## BEDDING...*IMPORTANT!*

Get in the habit of washing your bedsheets and pillowcases. They get oily and gross very quickly, which can lead to acne or mattress fermentation.

Wash these guys on warm or hot every week or two to get those oils out. Nothing feels better than sleeping in some freshly cleaned sheets. Try not to go to bed sweaty and gross.

## 2.10 FOOD

The freshman fifteen is a real thing for many people. If you're surprised you're gaining weight when you booze it up four nights a week and make 2:00 a.m. Tbell runs every time, don't be. Your food choices and habits can make a big difference in how you feel every day and how you perform in the classroom (or on the field, if you're an athlete). Take care of yourself.

If you chose a smaller meal plan and will consistently need sustenance from outside sources, you most likely have a few other options. See below.

FRESHMAN 15

## PRO TIPS

If you only need a few meals outside of your campus meal plan per week, fast food may be the cheaper go-to. Fast food doesn't mean junk food. Don't waste your money on McDonald's. For a dollar more than a McDonald's meal, you can get a burrito packed with great calories and nutrition.

If you need a lot of food outside of your meal plan, groceries, done right, can save you a bunch of money. That being said, buying groceries for one can be difficult. Figure out how much you can actually eat, and don't buy any more.

Where you shop can double the price or cut it in half. Don't shop at Whole Foods. Save that for when you're forty and boring and have nothing better to do with your money than blowing it on "high-class" food.

# CHAPTER 3: SKOO'

HOW TO KILL IT ACADEMICALLY

YOU DON'T NEED TO BE A GENIUS—JUST MAKE SMARTER DECISIONS.

## 3.1 TIME MANAGEMENT INFO

We firmly believe that time management is the most important skill set to acquire and use in college. If you're good at managing your time, then you're already ahead of the game. If not, you need to learn these skills to be successful.

You will not be in class for eight hours a day as you were in high school, with a sport or club meeting following immediately afterward. You will have larger blocks of time during the day at your disposal, and *you* can decide how to use these. The freedom to choose is a beautiful thing. Don't ruin it.

Making the wrong decisions with your time will actually take away your freedom in other areas of life. You don't want to have to turn down an invite for a night out with your friends because you have a paper to finish. You don't want to be forced to stay up all night because you're behind on studying for an exam in the morning. You'll find that being disciplined with your time on a daily basis will open up all sorts of new freedoms and opportunities. You can only be a "yes-man" if you know the appropriate times to say no.

Bottom line? *Get things done when there's less fun going on.*

# PRO TIPS

*Use a planner.* Whether it's a calendar on your phone, a physical assignment notebook, or something else, find a system that works. You want one place where you can keep track of assignments, exam dates, and deadlines. We've found that this makes a huge difference in managing stress. You don't have to worry about forgetting things if they're all written down in front of you. Your mother no longer manages your life.

Write out a schedule/to-do list before you go to bed. Plan what you have to accomplish the next day before you can relax. Stick to it.

Don't "stop" at your dorm room after class before going to the library/somewhere else to study. You want to sit down for twenty minutes and put your feet up after being in lecture all day—I get it. Next thing you know, you've been in your dorm room for two hours playing your roommate in NHL 15 and have forty bucks on the line. When you lose, you'll be pissed off and unable to focus during your night in the library, which is just getting started for you at six o'clock. If you'd gone straight there, you could be on your way home already.

Don't watch Netflix religiously. This can eat away your afternoon hours (or precious hours of sleep, if you watch in bed). We'd recommend deleting your account, at least for your first semester.

Friday afternoons are important. People tend to possess two mentalities:

1. Thank God it's the weekend. Let's booze as soon as class is over.

2. I have a whole afternoon free. I'm going to check out what I have to finish by Monday. Putting in just two hours of studying on Friday afternoon can make your weekend amazing. Why? You'll have peace of mind from knowing what you have to accomplish and how long it may take, instead of dreading opening your backpack on Sunday night. Most assignments take longer than you think they will. Get a head start so you're not forced to stay up all night on Sunday.

If you have a job, Friday afternoons are a great time to put some hours in.

Don't sleep until noon. Get up and going. A head start on your day feels a hell of a lot better than playing catch-up all day.

At our school, Thursdays were the night to go out. I had class Friday at 8:00 a.m. both semesters freshman year. I had many exams on Fridays, but I still wanted to go out and have fun with everyone Thursday nights. I made sure to study Monday, Tuesday, and Wednesday for my exams, and if I felt prepared, I'd go out and have a blast Thursday, then show up in the morning feeling like a champ because all the losers in there had stayed up all night studying while I'd been wheelin' and dealin'. This was the best strategy around. Not only was I confident going in to all those exams, but I also knew the material very well—better than all the "good students" who had been in the library all night.

### FINAL THOUGHTS

Buckle down. Get your shit done so you can have fun. Do things in the right order, and you'll find yourself with more time to do what you want.

# 3.2 LIFE IN A COLLEGE CLASSROOM

The college classroom is a different environment from what you were used to in high school. First thing to keep in mind: you're in the classroom because you paid for it. You pay for that professor's kid's friggin' violin lessons. Don't be so intimidated.

What does this mean? It means that you can leave the lecture to drop the kids off at the pool whenever you may need to. It means you can leave because you're bored. It means you can scroll through your phone in the back row the whole time. It means you might not have to show up.

It's nice to be done with the whole high school teacher–discipline deal, but your new freedom comes with a need for responsibility.

Your professor/TA most likely is not going to hold you accountable for showing up to class—that's on you. There's no one trying to babysit you or spoon-feed you the material; you have to find a way to get things done on your own or make the effort to reach out to others if you need help.

## PRO TIPS

Even if attendance isn't mandatory, missing several lectures can make passing your class difficult in the long run. We suggest attending every lecture you can. If they aren't helpful, study on your own during the lectures.

Participate once per class. It'll show your prof that you're interested and will help keep you engaged.

Don't waste your fellow students' time by chatting away with your professor throughout the lecture. No one likes the kid who won't stop asking questions.

Counting the professor's nose hairs doesn't do you any good. Take notes, stay engaged, and use your class time to your academic advantage. Think of it as studying on your own with a guide in the front of the room.

Because you are paying for your education, choosing to waste class time is a waste of your money. We did the math for our university. Divided throughout the semester, each lecture costs about $100. Think about that next time you're tempted to sleep in and skip.

## • STORY TIME •

During my first lecture in college, the girl across from me pulled out her phone and sent a text right in front of the professor's face. I was blown away. Was anyone else watching this happen? This girl had quite the set of balls! It was only a matter of time before the professor yelled at her for being so disrespectful. Boy, how wrong I was… he didn't care at all.

# 3.3 PROFESSOR RELATIONSHIPS

Establishing a relationship with your professor can help you in huge ways. Most of your professors will actually be cool people, especially if you've been using your newly acquired ratemyprofessor skills.

Nothing bad can happen from getting to know them more, as far as we know. A lot of good can.

Professors can hook you up with a research job, lead you to change your major, help you out with homework/projects/exams, excuse you from late penalties, recommend you to employers, write letters of recommendation for you, and introduce you to hoity-toity, important people.

## • STORY TIME •

Junior year, I took a materials-engineering class from a certain professor. I loved the class, studied hard, and showed her that I was genuinely interested in the material. I did nothing special, really. A few visits to her office hours and asking some questions in class were my only interactions with her. I did pretty well, and when I turned in my last exam, she pulled me aside and asked if I'd be interested in doing research for her. That professor is now my wife. (The previous sentence is not true.)

I went on to make some money working on a research project for her. Eventually, she became my academic adviser, and I decided to pursue a minor in material-science engineering under her. This never would've happened unless she thought I was extremely attractive. (The previous sentence is probably not true.) Moral of the story: put in a little effort with your professor, and you may reap some serious benefits.

# 3.4 STUDYING

Many students are halfway through college before they figure out how to study effectively. Everyone has his own way of learning, and no universal secret will make you ace all your classes. We're going to throw a bunch of tips that have been effective for us your way, and we challenge you to try a handful of them.

# PRO TIPS

Don't just study for your exams. Information builds from lecture to lecture, course to course, and year to year. If you're cramming the night before, just hoping to pass an exam, it's much harder to understand and retain the material. Take fifteen minutes after lectures in your classes to rewrite your notes or look over them.

Don't study in your dorm room. You'll encounter too many distractions: food, TV, invites to go do things. Remove yourself.

Studying with friends or classmates is tempting. Often these study groups turn into hanging out without getting much done. Studying with others can be very beneficial, and they can help you learn, but unless you need direct help from others or they need you, study alone. If you want to study with friends, throw your headphones on and focus on what you're working on.

If you're in the library or some other quiet spot, remember that studying is the reason you're there. Put your phone on airplane mode or put it in your backpack. Get in, get it done, get out, and have fun. Approach your to-do list with a hard-hat mentality, and don't let anything distract you from it. No need to waste your time if you're already in that dreaded library.

Frequency of study sessions is more powerful than duration. Space out your studying in multiple sessions, revisiting material and refreshing your mind on it. You'll find yourself retaining and understanding more information this way. It is difficult to understand a month of lectures after one sitting, even if it lasts ten hours.

When studying for exams, make study guides. If your prof provides them, fill them out. He or she is literally giving you the answers indirectly. Focus on understanding the big-picture themes of a class before narrowing down to topics you need to learn/practice.

Cut unnecessary corners. Sometimes skipping the readings or small assignments can work to your benefit. Time is money. Find out what information is important and focus on it.

No all-nighters. Lack of sleep screws with your head. You'll find yourself forgetting easy stuff on the exam the next morning with a fried brain.

Make a reward system for yourself. For each chapter you read or assignment you complete, treat yourself to a snack, a five-minute break, or whatever you need for some extra motivation.

Figure out how you learn! Are you a visual, oral, or practical learner? Find out your strategy and play to your strengths. If you're going to spend two hours reading and retain none of it, don't do it. Find another way to learn the information.

Plan time blocks when you are going to study, and stick to them. Don't just assume that you'll find time somewhere to finish your assignment.

# 3.5 ONLINE CLASSES & COMMUNITY COLLEGE

Taking classes online or through a local community college has the potential to save you even more money than a financial-aid reward or an outside scholarship does.

Our school's cost for a standard, four-credit class was $4,500 (before factoring in scholarship money). Taking a general class that fulfills one of your graduation requirements might cost you less than $1,000 outside of your university. That's $3,500 you and your family could save. Courses taken online or at a community college may also be easier.

Some schools limit the number of credits that students can transfer from outside institutions and still receive their diploma. For example, within my major, I could transfer in only eight credits from outside institutions. The rest had to come from my own engineering department. Depending on your school's rules, you may be allowed to transfer more credits for general curriculum courses.

## PRO TIPS

Find out what your school's credit-transfer policy is. Determine which classes in your intended major and/or general courses you may be able to transfer from another institution.

# 3.6 FINAL EXAMS

We do not want you to be intimidated by final exams.

Believe it or not, finals week was my favorite time of the semester. I may have lost some credibility with you with that previous sentence. I'm not that nerdy—let me explain.

During finals week, you probably won't have your normal lectures to sit through, leaving plenty of time to study on your own and get your life in order. If done right, everything from the semester can start to make a ton of sense and tie together during this week, which can be a cool feeling. If you take control of your time and study schedule, you can be prepared to kill these exams.

## PRO TIPS

Stay organized, course by course and chapter by chapter. Again, know the big-picture themes of your class. Tie them together before zooming in on each topic. Find out what you need to know for your exam before wasting time elsewhere.

Study ahead in small doses. You don't want to cram a semester's worth of material into one night. Save your study materials from the previous exams in each class to use when preparing for the final. Make a study guide weeks ahead of time if your professor isn't going to provide one.

Create a full schedule for finals week, planning out exam days/times and when you are going to study for them. Don't be overwhelmed when you see four exams in one week. Study one subject at a time and then move on to the next.

In theory, you should have learned most of the material already (if it is a cumulative exam). Revisit what you know for a refresher, and then focus on things you still need work on.

Once again: frequent study sessions are better one massive study session the night before the exam. Revisit the information regularly, and it'll be second nature.

## FINAL THOUGHTS

I'm no whiz at all, and I was fine during four years of engineering final exams while working and playing a sport. Staying organized, focusing on the big-picture themes of each class, and planning ahead will pay off.

# 3.7 STUDY DRUGS

Adderall, Ritalin, Vyvanse—the list goes on. So-called "study drugs" are developed and prescribed for people with attention deficit disorder. Basically, these meds influence the brain in a way that helps you focus.

Our generation was pretty much raised in an environment that conditioned an attention deficit within us. We expect everything to be easy, efficient, and instantaneous because a few touches on our smartphones can get us anything we want. Because of this conditioning, sitting down and studying one subject for four hours does not come easily to most of us. You'll need long periods of focus to get things done at school. Many people who are not diagnosed with ADD resort to these pills (Adderall, most commonly) as a study buddy.

Unless your doctor prescribed them to you, we would advise against taking study drugs.

Here's why:

- **They can be extremely addictive.** You may feel like you can cure cancer when taking them. It's easy to start to crave the feeling or ability they can provide. If you get in a habit of taking them, you may start to depend on them to get anything done. Bad.

- **It's easy to become dependent.** If you get in a habit of taking them, you may feel the need to keep doing so to get anything done. That is not a good thing.

- **There are side effects.** Loss of appetite, trouble falling asleep, and mood swings are the most common.

- **It's a felony.** Selling/possessing someone else's prescription drugs is illegal AF.

If you do end up taking Adderall, which we advise against, we don't want you to be miserable.

## PRO TIPS

Approach with caution. Realize that this is a prescription drug you're dealing with. It's a felony, bruh.

"XRs" are extended release; you'll feel their effects for eight to twelve hours. "IRs" are instant release. You'll feel their effects for four to six hours.

Do not take study drugs late in the day. There's a good chance they'll mess up your sleep schedule.

Make sure to eat. Your appetite may be nonexistent. Don't trust it.

Eliminate distractions and plan out what you need to do during the extent of the effects. If you get sidetracked while under the influence, you may end up knitting your dog a new winter sweater. And you don't even knit.

### FINAL THOUGHTS

*Use it well.*

–*Sirius Black*

# CHAPTER 4: OH, HOLY NIGHT

NIGHTLIFE LESSONS

## 4.1 DRINKING/TIPS

Drinking is fun. Hangovers are not.

Let's start off with a little rant:

No one gives a shit about how many shots you took.

You don't have to be blackout drunk to be the life of the party.

Stop convincing yourself that you have to be drunk to talk to women. Grow a sack. It's attractive to be confident in your own skin.

If you can't control yourself and seem to really screw things up every time you get drunk, stop getting so drunk. The consequences of your actions are real, no matter how intoxicated you are.

## PRO TIPS

Mix in water. Dehydration from boozing is hard on your body. Every few hours, chug a glass of water.

Don't keep drinking after 1:00 a.m. There's little to gain and more to lose at that point. Thank your drunk self tomorrow.

Know your limits. There will come a time where you're already shit-faced and someone passes you a bottle. If saying no is too hard for you, throw it back and fake a few gulps. It's better than spending half of your morning bent over the toilet.

Beer > hard liquor. Light beer is the king of good nights and mild hangovers.

Find a morning-after routine that works for your body. Don't waste your whole day lying in bed until 3:00 p.m. and feeling sorry for yourself. Your hangover feels worse the longer you stay in bed. Get up, drink water, eat, workout...do anything to get on with your life. Try not to waste eight hours the next day on your four hours of fun the night before.

If you really feel the need to puke, pull the trigger. Listen to your body if it wants to get rid of all the shit sloshing around in your stomach.

The course of a night has a lot to do with your mentality going into it. If your mission is to get blackout drunk, you'll find a way to do it. If you're looking for a more casual night out with friends, you'll pace yourself. Know what you're trying to do and stick to it. Keep in mind what you have going on the next day.

### FINAL THOUGHTS

Know your drinking games. Youtube it up. For starters:
Beer pong • Flip cup • Quarters • Edward 40 Hands

(This may not apply in your state.)

Whether you have "legalize it" tattooed on your calf or you're a neoconservative wall-builder who thinks marijuana is Satan's direct presence on this earth, let's talk about weed.

First off, it's not for everyone. A lot of people simply don't like the feeling. That being said, if you choose not to smoke, there's no need to be an asshole about other people smoking. Their decisions do not affect you—unless you're going to get in trouble directly because of them.

## PRO TIPS

If you do find yourself a-blazin', here is our advice in terms of your personal safety and evasion of authorities.

Know the laws concerning cannabis in your state. Keep them in mind when making decisions. Risk/reward.

Find a dealer you know and trust. Don't pick up from some sketchball who doesn't give a shit about you besides what's in your wallet. You want to know what you're smoking.

Do not smoke in the dorms. No matter how hard you try to suppress or cover up the smell, it still smells. Easy giveaway. Go for a walk, or find an off-campus place where it'll be safer.

Storage: airtight and out of sight. You're better off keeping your goodies at a friend's house or apartment.

After smoking, chew some gum and wash your hands. Your breath and your fingers are the most likely to smell after the fact. Don't overdo it with AXE—you're not in sixth grade.

Do not carry weed on you, especially after smoking, when you might smell. We'd recommend joints instead of smoking from pipes or bongs. Limit the evidence.

### FINAL THOUGHTS

Everything in moderation. No one who gets caught thought they were going to get caught.

# 4.3 HOUSE PARTY

So you're going to your first college house party. Congratulations, young buck. You should know a few things concerning you, the hosts, and safety.

When I was growing up in Wisconsin, an underage-consumption ticket was no biggie — it was just like paying an expensive parking ticket. When I came to Minnesota, everyone was always freaking out about getting a "minor" (consumption ticket). While at school, getting caught underage was a much bigger deal legally and could stay on your criminal record for a while. Find out what your state drinking laws are.

## PRO TIPS

If you happen to run into the host(s), ntroduce yourself and thank them for havin' a shindig. It's a big pain to clean up after a party, and they're risking getting themselves in trouble by having underage homies over. Get to know them, and maybe return the favor someday.

Don't show up with a tribe of ten dudes. No group of guys hosting a party wants a sausage fest all night. If you can't go with girls, keep it to two or three of your brohans when you show up at the door.

Be respectful of the house. Don't steal stuff. Don't break stuff. Make sure your friends aren't doing stupid shit.

Bring your own booze. Don't bank on mooching all night. If you are empty-handed, bring some cash to offer people if they give you a beer or five. Pay for the keg if the guy collecting money is bigger than you.

Know the environment. Are you in a residential neighborhood surrounded by normal human beings? Are you right by campus with college houses on the whole street? If you can hear the party from a block away on your way there, so can the neighbors. Depending on its location, you may want to turn around.

Locate the nearest exit. Have an escape plan if the coppas do show up.

Pick someone you promise to leave with at the end of the night unless you hear otherwise. It seems like every year, a student dies after walking home alone and passing out somewhere or getting lost when it's cold out. Especially if you live in a cold climate, keep track of your friends. If you won't do it for yourself, do it for your mother. And theirs.

## 4.4 FAKE IDs & BOUNCERS

Bars are fun, but twenty-one is old. False identification sometimes can get you in before you're of age.

Four out of six of my current roommates have worked in a college bar. I was a bouncer, two others were bouncers, and the fourth managed the bar. So yes, we have some advice when it comes to trying to get in.

### PRO TIPS

In-state hand-me-downs are far better than fake IDs. Bouncers know a fake when they see one.

If you know an older student who looks somewhat like you and is from the state your school is located in, ask if you can buy his ID from him. Chances are he can go online or take a trip to the DMV to buy a new one.

Memorize your shit. If it's fake or doesn't look like you, or if you look young, they may question you at the door. Know the information on your ID like the back of your hand and be confident upon interrogation. Know your state capital, house address, governor's name, and other random facts about your ID's state. Pick a high school name and mascot. (The capital of Illinois is not Chicago.)

Bouncers likely will know you are underage, even if they decide to let you in. If a bar is known to be more lenient about letting in underagers, the thought going through the bouncer's head will be, *Is this kid going to be a problem?* It's often in your power to answer this question for him. Dress maturely. Act maturely. Don't roll up to the door drunk as hell. Be composed and confident.

When you walk up to the bouncer, strike up a conversation. Ask how his night's been going. Nothing screams "I just got my first pube" louder than you standing awkwardly, your legs shaking and voice trembling while he examines your ID.

If possible, have a second form of ID at the ready (e.g., a health-insurance card or credit card). Leave it in your wallet. Don't take it out right away. Doing so tells bouncers that something is sketchy, so present it only if they ask to see it.

Don't show up with a squad of five guys. A bouncer is much likelier to let in an underage guy who's with five girls. The ratio in a bar is important to the bouncers and the bartenders. They want ladies in there just as much as you do. Sausage fests are not ideal for business.

Get denied? Take it like a man. Be respectful and leave—they did their job. Do not put up an argument. You are not going to convince them that your fake ID is real. They literally get paid to deny guys like you, so don't start whining about it. You're better off walking away and hoping the bouncer forgets your face; that way, you can give it another try another weekend.

If the bouncer takes your ID, you can respectfully ask to have it back, but don't be surprised if he keeps it. Some bouncers may give it back for some cash if you're that desperate to keep it.

Getting to know bouncers over time is a good way to help your chances. If you do end up becoming friends, don't text a bouncer to ask when he is working or whether he'll let you and your friends in. He'll hate it.

## FINAL THOUGHTS

Accept defeat. Even if you are twenty-one, bouncers have the right to deny anyone service. Don't give them a reason to.

## 4.5 BAR ETIQUETTE

You made it in. Imagine a house party with no risk of cops. College bars can be a great time…but also a black hole for your wallet.

First things first. If you make awful decisions every time you visit, don't go. If you can't handle yourself in a bar, you may end up with two black eyes, a negative balance in your bank account, or a night in jail.

You should know a few things concerning your behavior during a night at the bar. Don't be clueless in this new environment, further proving your underagedness.

Drunk guy 1

VS

Drunk guy 2

## PRO TIPS

**With bartenders, time is money.**

Your goal is probably to get a drink. What's the best way to do this in an overcrowded bar where everyone else wants to do the same? Prove to the bartender that you'll be a fast and painless customer.

Use cash. Bartenders hate credit cards, which take far longer to process. Hold out your cash so they can see what you're paying with. Don't shove it in their faces, and don't yell at them. Patiently wait with cash in hand. Also, if you only bring cash and leave the credit card at home, you will not wake up with a $200 tab on your bank statement.

Know what you're going to order. When they finally make it to you, if you don't know what you want, they might just walk away. Don't make them wait for you.

Tip a dollar per drink. If you want them to like you or serve you first next time, throw them a five.

## ETIQUETTE

Bars are crowded. It's part of the game. Don't be the douchebag who fights a guy because he bumped into you. This is the classic case of I-have-no-self-worth-and-probably-a-tiny-penis-and-must-compensate-with-overagressive-actions. You most likely will not be welcomed back to a bar you fought at.

Do not bring in your own booze. A bar is literally a free party unless you choose to buy a drink (or there is a cover charge). Respect that.

If you are completely plastered, it is better to take a cab home early than to make a fool of yourself and puke in the bar. No shame in throwing in the towel.

## WOMEN

If you want to strike up a conversation with a certain someone, keep it simple. "Can I buy you a drink?" will suffice. Don't be creepy. No means no.

Have your female friends introduce you to a girl you're interested in. You'll have more of a chance at a conversation than if you approach her on your own.

Don't be afraid to go up to a girl, even if she's with friends. She might be more flattered if you single her out around other girls. Introduce yourself and be a gentleman.

Do not take girls home who are absolutely blackout drunk. That's messed up. Turn off your horny, primitive little brain for ten seconds. Think about what you are doing before you leave with someone. Never buy a girl more than two drinks.

Simply put, being a very attractive girl in a college bar would suck. A lot. All night they have sloppy drunk dudes grabbing them and spitting as they try to put together sentences. Don't be one of those guys. If you're actually interested in her, be mature, respectful, and have the balls to talk to her before you get hammered.

# CHAPTER 5: WHEELS

ADVICE FOR YOUR LOVE LIFE

## 5.1 THE HIGH SCHOOL GIRLFRIEND

If you are single going into your first semester, skip to the next chapter.

Before we get started, if you don't see yourself potentially ending up with this woman with whom you are in a relationship, save yourself. End it now, and move on to the next chapter after this paragraph. Trust us—staying with your high school girlfriend is not worth the time, stress, or sacrifice a relationship demands unless you 100 percent see a future with the gal.

### DISTANCE

If you've been with your significant other for quite some time and you do see a future with her, staying together is worth a try.

It will suck. We're not going to sugarcoat it.

Relationships are pretty much the shared feelings and experiences you have with someone else, right? If you two are going to be eight hours apart, shared experiences are tough to come by. Your relationship will be based on trust and communication if you aren't able to see each other. *Trust and communication.* You will not stay together if you don't have these things nailed down.

Before leaving for school, you need to have some serious talks with your SO.

- What are your expectations for each other?

- What do you need from her to feel comfortable with the state of your relationship (and vice versa)?

- What if things go south and you break up?

- Why are you going to put yourselves through this? Is it worth it?

Remaining in a long-distance relationship will be a struggle. Jealousy is (h)uuuuuge, as President Donald might say. Your lady is going to see girls in your Snapchat and jump to conclusions—and vice versa. Even if you trust each other, doubts and worries will creep into your head at some point. Your thoughts may become negative, and you'll assume the worst. Read *Evolution of Desire* to better understand jealousy in a relationship. Shit's natural.

## PRO TIPS

Don't be afraid to connect with your lady friends and cultivate friendships, but hang tight. Don't date right away.

If you're interested in someone, maybe you could let her know but say that you promised yourself you wouldn't settle down with anyone freshman year. If she can't handle waiting a few short months for you, she's probably not the one anyway.

My roommate was in a long-distance relationship with his high school sweetheart throughout college, and his input was very helpful:

- There's a huge difference between one, two, and eight hours away. (You might be able to see her during a day trip if she's nearby but only a few times a year if she's not.)

- Even if you totally trust her, you will be troubled by some situations, and doubts will creep into your head.

- Small bothers will turn into tragedies. Sometimes you just need to stay cool and sleep it off.

- College changes people. It will change you and your lady. Don't expect her to remain the same person she was in high school.

- Being in a long-distance relationship can be a blessing in disguise. You can focus on school, guy friends, and hobbies, and it makes the time you end up spending with your significant other even more special.

**High school relationships continuing at the same school:**

If you and your high school significant other end up at the same school, dope. Attending the same college is an awesome experience to share with someone special. That being said, many of our tips still apply.

Don't let your relationship keep you from branching out in other aspects of your college life. Meet as many people as you can, have your own friends and hobbies, and try to thrive independently. Don't let your daily life and college experience become completely dependent on your lady…what if you break up?

If you do break up, try to take the high road. Be respectful throughout the process. You will regret calling her a bitch to all your friends. If you're going to be on the same campus for four years, we'd recommend trying to end it on good terms.

## 5.2 NO A$AP WIFEY

If you're starting school single, we advise against getting into a serious relationship during freshman year. Here's why:

First off, you don't really know people yet, even if you think you do. As I said before, everyone is nice, friendly, and fun when school starts—they need to make friends in their new environment. Some people don't show their true colors until later, when they have established their friend groups. Even if you think some gal is amazing, she may be putting on a temporary mask.

Second, committing to a relationship comes with sacrifices. You're less likely to branch out, try new things, and make new friends if you're hanging out with a certain someone all day. Freshman year is not the time to say no to these other opportunities.

---

### PRO TIPS

Don't be afraid to connect with your lady friends and cultivate friendships, but hang tight. Don't date right away.

If you're interested in someone, maybe you could let her know but say that you promised yourself you wouldn't settle down with anyone freshman year. If she can't handle waiting a few short months for you, she's probably not the one anyway.

## 5.3 DATING

Chivalry is not dead. Yes, hookup culture is becoming more of the norm at many schools, but don't think that's all there is.

If you're genuinely interested in someone, ask her on a date. Don't just slide into her DMs, talk to her only when you're drunk on the weekend, or resort to telling her friends you're interested. These are a coward's ways out of pursuing someone. "Be a man" is a phrase our generation is constantly scrutinizing, but this is a situation where I feel it's appropriate. Be a man and ask her out. When you're both sober.

Don't say, "Hey, you want to hang out sometime?" She'll assume Netflix and chill. Boring brohans who have nothing exciting to offer a gal resort to Netflix and chilling on a first date. Don't be a boring brohan. Ask her to do something specific, simple, and quick. Don't spend a full day on a first date. Have a fixed end time. Take her out for coffee or go to a sports game—something casual. Don't put a ton of pressure on it; just enjoy the time getting to know her. If you want to keep it even more casual, invite her to a night out with your friends.

### PRO TIPS

Grow a sack and ask her out.

Phone calls > texts. Don't hide behind your fat thumbs. Do not slide into someone's DMs unless it's the only possible means of communication.

Use your closer female friends as a resource. They'll have good advice for you in your specific pursuit, if you need it.

If she says no, get on with your life. Now you don't have to worry about her anymore.

# 5.4 STARTIN' A 'SHIP IN COLLEGE

If you happen to kick off a relationship with a lucky lady, we have some advice for you. From experience.

College is both an awesome and a difficult time to be in a serious relationship. People are changing and don't always have their shit together. You might be making big life decisions. A college campus is a very strong environment of sexual temptation, considering proximity, alcohol, lack of discipline, and so on.

## PRO TIPS

Don't put a ton of pressure on the state of your relationship. Don't think too hard about it or sweat the little things. Relationships come and go; she's not your end-all. You're young, and there are many other women out there if things don't work out.

Don't let your relationship take over your life. Don't let your woman distract you from killing it in school, pursuing your interests, and making friends. Manage and balance your time with her.

If you lose your friendships because you spend all your time with her, you'll have no friends if you break up. If you end up staying together, you'll still have no friends.

### FINAL THOUGHTS

If you start a relationship, take care of yourself and proceed with caution. Don't lose sight of the other aspects of your life.

# 5.5 "CASUAL"

If you're looking not for a relationship but for more casual encounters, we ask you to keep a few things in mind.

# PRO TIPS

College is not Blue Mountain State. Don't assume everyone wants to sleep with you.

The "success" of your night is not dependent on whom you go home with. That's just setting yourself up to be a disappointed douchebag.

Respecting girls is tight. Consent is sexy. And 100 percent necessary. If she's intoxicated, do the right thing.

Reason #1: Have some friggin' dignity.

Reason #2: Guys are defenseless in sexual-assault accusations, even if completely innocent. Never put yourself in a sticky situation even if you have angelic intentions.

Just because you're a guy, it doesn't mean you have to dish out the D to anyone who's interested. Know where you stand before the opportunity comes. Be happy with the decisions you make.

Don't hook up with your ex.

Be straightforward and honest. If you're not interested in anything serious, don't lead her to believe so.

Please don't hook up with your good friends. Doing so can ruin that friendship and your whole friend group.

If you hook up with a girl and see her on campus later, don't ignore her existence. Be friendly and say hello. If you're embarrassed, she probably is too.

Don't share all the details with your friends. Respect her privacy.

STDs are real. Also babies. Be smart and safe. Don't let one night define the rest of your life.

If you see someone being harassed (contrary to popular feminist belief, this happens to men, too) do something about it. Sexual assault is a real problem where a human (like you) can actually step in to help someone in need.

# CHAPTER 6: COLLEGE LIFE TOPICS

THIS CHAPTER DOES NOT HAVE A SPECIFIC THEME. IT'S MORE OF A COLLECTION OF TOPICS THAT MAY COME UP DURING YOUR FRESHMAN YEAR AND BEYOND.

## 6.1 CAMPUS POLICE

Being a dick to your campus safety officers does not work in your favor. Yelling at them, talking back to them, and being difficult to work with may lead them to screw you over. Don't be like that.

Campus police vary significantly from school to school in their roles, behaviors, and abilities. Some are more like extensions of your state police force. Some are less-qualified twenty-two-year-olds who dream of wearing the real badge someday.

**Why should you cooperate with them?**

They can help you out. Maybe you're locked out of your dorm room or need a ride home late at night.

They decide whether to get you in trouble. Don't make them want to.

Even if you're caught doing something illegal, be honest, calm, apologetic, and mature. They might let things slide.

Their main priority is not to catch a freshman who's a little buzzed. It's to keep you and the entire student body safe.

Everyone already hates them, and they know it. No reason to add to it. Be respectful, and they'll respect you in return. Use "sir" and "ma'am" when addressing them.

# 6.2 PHYSICAL HEALTH

Your body is a temple. As far as we know, it's the only one you get.

The biggest challenge is getting into a habit of making physical health a priority. I'm not just talking about getting yoked for the ladies. It's about making the decision to love your body and take control of it. It's one of the very few things in this life that you actually have some level of control over, so why not take advantage?

Refusing to take care of your body can have some serious consequences. Getting sick in college sucks balls. It's not like high school, when it's dope to skip school while your friends are stuck there all day. You still have to get your stuff done. Profs won't feel bad for you. Especially in the dorms, which are incubators for spreading illnesses, it is very easy to fall under the weather.

## • STORY TIME •

Making healthy choices will not affect everyone to the same extent. One of my roommates ate pizza and drank four Mountain Dews every day, didn't work out much, and stayed up until 3:00 a.m. playing video games every night. The guy was a 140-pound computer engineer, a manager at a local bar, and a total baller. Maybe you're one of the lucky ones who isn't affected much by living a physically "unhealthy" lifestyle, but for many, making good choices can make a world of a difference in your daily life.

## PRO TIPS

Most of us know what food is good for us and what isn't. If you don't, I'd recommend doing some reading. It's up to you to monitor and balance your diet. Don't pound cheeseburgers every day at the cafeteria. Your brain and the rest of your body need good fuel to function correctly.

Whether it's for you or the ladies, we strongly recommend exercising often. The human body isn't meant to be a couch potato. Lift, run, play sports—do whatever you can to stay in shape. If you consistently mix in workouts, chances are you'll find yourself more alert, motivated, and focused throughout your days.

### FINAL THOUGHTS

Physical health is dependent on your diet, exercise, and sleep.
Sleep deserves its own chapter (6.3).

My book recommendations for physical health include *The 4-Hour Body* by Tim Ferris and *In Defense of Food* by Michael Pollan.

# 6.3 SLEEP

A common saying is that there are three priorities you can have in college—school, partying, and sleep—and you have to pick two. We'd recommend against dismissing sleep as a priority.

Trying to live on unhealthy sleep habits can really mess with your body, screw up your brain, and make you sick. I got sick all the time my freshman year after going through a weekend on two or three hours of sleep. You have to make sleep a priority. You don't want your lack of sleep bringing you down academically, socially, or physically.

Sleep is a difficult beast to conquer in college for several reasons. Chances are you won't start and end your days at the same times routinely. You may have your sleep schedule interrupted by loud roommates or their alarms. You might be behind on your studying and think you should spend half the night in the library, sacrificing precious hours of rest.

## PRO TIPS

Listen to your body. Take a nap if you need it. Go to bed early and stay ahead of the game.

Download a sleep-cycle app on your phone. These track your sleeping patterns and wake you up during your lightest sleep, leaving you feeling more naturally rested and awake.

An extra few hours of sleep may be more beneficial than extra hours of studying the night before an exam. If your brain is exhausted, it is very difficult to perform, even if you are prepared.

If you're not a morning person, do some push-ups, sit-ups, and squats as soon as you roll out of bed. Get the blood flowing. You'll find yourself walking taller and feeling less groggy all morning.

# 6.4 MENTAL HEALTH

Just as your physical health is important, you need to take care of yourself mentally.

If you're suffering from depression, homesickness, or any personal struggle, seek help! Meet with a counselor at your school. People are there for you.

## PRO TIPS

Use the resources available to you at your school and online—be a consumer. Get advice and share your struggles with people who can help you. If you try something or someone and it doesn't help you out, continue on with the next option available.

Journal. It's a great way to have a date with yourself. Learn from your mistakes, behaviors, and daily mind-set. Have fun with it. Write down your memories from the weekend. It's crazy how much you forget in a short period. I love looking back at my journals from freshman/sophomore years and seeing what I was thinking and doing. And yes, I will read that shit to my grandkids.

Find a mentor. It's a great idea to have someone you trust who can give you advice, keep you on track, and listen if you need to vent.

### FINAL THOUGHTS

You're responsible for knowing where you're at. Check in with yourself. Put in the effort to get help, a lot of people are in the same boat.

Reading Suggestion: *You're a Badass* by Jen Sincero

# 6.5 FAITH

Our guess is that many of you grew up in a home atmosphere that incorporated some aspect of faith or spirituality.

Our advice? Don't run from it quite yet.

Yes, you're on your own. Yes, you now get to decide things for yourself. Many people see this as their opportunity to ditch their faith altogether, as they're not being forced to go to church or live a certain lifestyle anymore. I'd like to challenge you to do otherwise.

## PRO TIPS

Whether you're atheist, Christian, Jewish, Muslim, etc, dig into the faith you were raised in. Question your beliefs. Maybe you should believe something not because your parents told you it was true but because you proved it to yourself. No matter what faith background you were raised in, college is a great opportunity to pursue it on your own.

Find friends and organizations on campus to continue the conversation with or to support you in your spiritual journey.

Read. Watch documentaries. Gather information. If you don't know what you believe, this is a great time to make an effort to find out!

### FINAL THOUGHTS

Just as college is a chance to make new friends, it is an awesome gift of a fresh start on the spiritual side of things. Now is a time when you can start thinking and developing spiritual questions/answers on your own

Reading Suggestions: *Reason for God* by Tim Keller
*The God Delusion* by Richard Dawkins

# 6.6 PERSONAL TIME

Do you find yourself getting frustrated with your friends? Is your roommate pissing you off? Are you way too stressed out with school? Take some time to treat yo'self.

## PRO TIPS

Remove yourself from the atmosphere that's bugging you. Take a full day to be on your own, work out, study, read, and watch your favorite show. Don't have FOMO (fear of missing out) or feel like you can't say no to your friends…have an awesome day on your own. Sometimes you have to do your own thing for a while.

Join a club that none of your friends is in. Pick a hobby that's your own, that no one can take from you. Don't ruin your newfound independence by depending on your friend group for everything.

## • STORY TIME •

My roommate had a weekly ritual of going to the same local restaurant, ordering a pizza and a beer, and reading for a few hours. A ritual like this can be a good way to recalibrate and check in with yourself. Treat yourself once a week.

## FINAL THOUGHTS

It is both unhealthy and unsustainable for your personal happiness to be fully reliant on your friends and their schedules.

# 6.7 EMPLOYMENT AS A FULL-TIME STUDENT

From our experience, a minimum-wage job that offers you nothing besides that $8.50 an hour is not worth your precious time.

Bold strategy, Cotton.

Let me explain. As a full-time student, you know that time is money. You don't want to waste your time earning next to nothing after taxes. When looking for employment, it's a decent time to embrace your friggin' inner millennial and believe you deserve more than just that hourly paycheck.

Ask yourself: What does this job offer me besides minimum wage?

## • STORY TIME •

I had an awesome experience as a valet at a local restaurant for two years. It was dope, and I got to test-drive every car out there. It was pretty much getting paid to go car shopping. I earned cash tips on top of minimum wage and ate an amazing meal at the end of every night.

## PRO TIPS

Find jobs that will provide you with more pay, solid work or life experience, possible networking exposure, skills, free food, the option to study while working, or a great title on your resume.

Put in the time to look around for all possible employment opportunities. Don't settle right away. Ask your friends from the area if they have any ideas or connections for you.

If your job makes you miserable, respectfully quit and find a new one. Even if you feel badly about letting your employer down, don't let guilt be the reason you stay if it's not a good fit.

After you accept a good job, ditch the millennial mentality. Work your balls off. Don't be a lazy-ass college kid. Show that you're grateful for the opportunity.

We'd recommend finding a serving job at a local restaurant. Find a place where you can earn lots in tips, eat a hot meal (free, ideally) at the end of your shift, and gain valuable customer-service experience.

# 6.8 DO SOMETHING ELSE

You need something besides school and your social life. Four years of only those two things will get old. Does it really sound fulfilling just to pass your classes and get hammered on the weekends every weekend for four years?

## • STORY TIME •

Playing a sport for my school was a huge outlet. If I was stressed out with school, frustrated with women, or sick of my friends, lacrosse was there for me to blow off some steam. Finding passion through my teammates and becoming a better player helped keep me sane in my everyday life.

## PRO TIPS

Play a sport. Volunteer. Start or join an organization, and invest yourself in it. Be a superfan for your school's teams. Start a business. Write a book ;)

There are incredible opportunities offered at universities for extracurriculars. Ours had a rock climbing club, where students could climb at a nearby gym on Friday nights for free ($40 value). Embrace your mooch.

These pursuits not only will be exciting and fun but may also add to your résumé.

Don't think school is your end-all. No one cares about your GPA. Chances are you have a lot more time now to pursue other interests than you will once you're a workin' man with kiddos.

## FINAL THOUGHTS

"I'm just trying to get through school."

"I'm a full-time student."

Going through college with these mentalities puts a ceiling on your potential—get rid of them.

# 6.9 OFF-CAMPUS LIVING

Why is living off campus discussed in a freshman-year advice book?

Depending on your school's housing culture, you may have to make some housing decisions toward the end of your first year at school. Most people sign leases for off-campus houses or apartments during spring semester of their freshman year. If living off campus for your sophomore year interests you, you need to start planning.

Sometimes, by the end of freshman year, guys are anxious to get off campus and get their own places. Campus police won't bother you, and you can choose your multiple roommates, have more freedom, throw parties, and so on. Living off campus brings exciting new freedoms, just as moving away to school for the first time does.

The on-/off-campus living decision can be a tough one. Here are some pros and cons to help you decide.

## LIVING ON CAMPUS

**Pros:**

It's convenient as hell. Living close to your cafeteria, gym, and classes is really nice.

Minimal responsibilities. Chances are your housing will be covered in one flat fee, and you won't have any other bills to deal with.

**Cons:**

Usually more expensive.

Increased odds of getting caught for drinking, doing drugs, or throwing a party.

## LIVING OFF CAMPUS

**Pros:**

Usually less expensive.

More freedom. No one's policing you...unless the actual police get involved.

**Cons:**

Usually not as convenient. If you end up in a house a twenty-minute walk away, you'll find that it's harder to drag yourself to campus for class, workouts, and any campus activities, especially in bad weather.

Additional responsibilities. You have to deal with landlords, utility bills, and some adult responsibilities such as shoveling snow, cutting your grass, and keeping track of your trash/recycling stuff.

## PRO TIPS

Compare the costs of staying on campus and moving off. Think about rent, food, transportation, and utilities.

Ask yourself what you want in your living space. Convenience and accessibility? Freedom to do illegal things without fear of getting caught? Sharing a room vs. having your own?

Do the research sooner rather than later. You want to have the freedom to choose your apartment/house/dorm rather than be forced to live in it because everything else is taken. At the start of second semester, make a decision with your friends about what you plan to do, and act on it.

Don't live farther than a fifteen-minute walk from campus, if possible.

Don't live with people you know you're not going to get along with. This may seem obvious, but it happens, and it usually doesn't work out.

If you decide to live off campus, make it a priority to develop a good relationship with your landlord. You'll need him or her for both fixing your house and not kicking you out of it.

## • STORY TIME •

Six of us lived in a house off campus for three years, and it was an awesome experience. We were a ten-minute walk from campus, had the freedom of having people over and doing illegal things, saved a ton of money on cheap rent, and felt like it was our own home. Living off campus was great for us, but we see how convenient it would be to still live on campus in the thick of things.

## 6.10 PHONES

*I got two phones: one for the plug, one for the load.*

–Kevin Gates

We don't want you to spend your entire college life staring at and caressing your phone. Yes, it is incredible that if you touch it in the right places in the right order, a pizza will show up at your door in thirty minutes. Shit's crazy, but your phone is a tool—not your identity.

## PRO TIPS

Don't let staring at your phone be the last thing you do before falling asleep and the first you do when you wake up.

Delete or deactivate social media during finals week. It's distracting AF.

Throw your phone in your backpack or set it to Do Not Disturb mode when studying.

Do not use it as the primary source of relationships. It's a great tool to get people together, but once you're hanging out, put your damn phone away. No one likes the kid at the party who's sitting on the couch and scrolling through Insta. Don't be him.

"Liking" girls' Instagram posts is a terrible way to express your interest in them. Talk to them. With your mouth.

# CHAPTER 7: YOU WILL GROW OLD

LONG-TERM ADVICE FOR THOSE WHO PLAN TO GRADUATE

## 7.1 RÉSUMÉ

A résumé is your report card for life. It is 100 percent necessary to make one for yourself, assuming you want a formal job someday.

Make a résumé during your freshman year if you don't have one already. Yes, it's most important right before graduation, when you'll likely be applying for big-boi jobs, but many employment opportunities/ internships during college will require you to submit a résumé and/or cover letter as well. It takes a long time to perfect your work of art. It's much easier to update a few things later on than to start from scratch when application deadlines are approaching.

Your school's career center will be an excellent resource. You most likely pay fees for these services in your tuition, so use them. Especially as you get closer to graduation, do not be afraid to set up an appointment with a career center adviser.

# 7.2 USE YOUR SUMMERS

Summers are very important periods in college. To use a sports analogy, summer is the off-season. You can use this valuable time to get better or waste it because you need "a break." Take advantage by getting ahead of the game.

We'd advise you to start building your résumé, make some serious money, or take classes during this time.

**INTERNSHIPS:**

How do you start building your résumé? Internships or jobs related to your (potential) major field are huge opportunities. You may gain valuable experience, money, and relationships. Paid or not, internships can help you narrow down your career-path options and open the door to other opportunities.

The younger you are, the better it is to start gaining valuable work experience. Sure, during the summer after freshman year, your friends may be running around getting baked and hitting every beach around your hometown. It's tempting to take the easy route, but again, we'd rather see you commit three months to something that may seriously pay off later.

Look for an internship related to your passion or field. Ask your professors if they have (or know of) any research opportunities over the summer. If they don't have any, they may be able to point you in the right direction. Did your parents ever tell you "the early bird gets the worm"? Be early.

Apply, apply, apply. Don't think that because you applied for two internships you'll get accepted to at least one. Not true at all. Apply to as many that may appeal to you as possible.

## PRO TIPS

If you land an internship, keep these things in mind:

You're there to learn. Ask as many questions as you can. Soak up all the information. Work hard. Show you care.

Establish solid relationships with your superiors and fellow interns. These are valuable networks that may come in handy when it's time to find a job. You may be asking your boss for a letter of recommendation in the future. He may be asking you to work for him.

If you do not end up with an internship, please still take advantage of your summer:

Job shadowing is a great way to explore what a career in a certain field may look like. Ask to shadow your parents' friends or coworkers. People will be happy to show you around for a half day and explain what they do.

Take classes. Maybe you need to in order to graduate "on time." Maybe you want to take one fewer course next semester in order to perform better or have more time to work during the fall and spring semesters. Taking summer classes can free up this time.

Travel or study abroad. See the next chapter for more details on this option.

## • STORY TIME •

My friend Lauren, a business major, was thinking about going into sports marketing. Lauren got an unpaid internship with a local professional sports team. She worked a ton of hours, and it turned her off from pursuing sports marketing completely. Was this a waste of time? Not at all. She found out that she didn't want to continue with sports marketing, thereby saving thousands on classes. That's much better than not interning and finding out that she hated sports marketing after graduating with a degree in it. On the other hand, if she had wanted to continue to work in that field, her internship would've enabled her to work for that team or other professional sports teams in the area. The connections and experience gained from internships can be incredibly valuable in the long run. Intern, intern, intern.

# 7.3 STUDY ABROAD

As we've said before, college is a time to expand your horizons. Many of us were raised to think of the good ole US of A as the only place in the world that matters. There's a lot more out there. Studying abroad during college will change your life. It's probably the best period in your life to go live somewhere else. (Most traditional college students don't have kids, a full-time job, a mortgage, or other similar obligations, after all.) It likely will be much harder later in life to live in another country for an extended period of time.

You can take classes for yet another normal semester on campus, or you could go live somewhere dope, learn a new language, get acclimated to another culture, and meet some amazing people from around the world. Which sounds cooler?

## • STORY TIME •

I had the amazing opportunity to live in Guatemala for the two summers before my junior and senior years. My prior internship experience in my field allowed me to accept this opportunity. While most of my peers were working full-time internships those two summers, I was learning how to build houses and speak Spanish in Central America. Incredible life experience. I can't imagine saying no to the opportunity at this point, but at the time, the idea scared me a little bit. Do the uncomfortable.

## PRO TIPS

If you create your four-year plan during freshman year, you'll find it much easier to fit studying abroad into your undergrad experience. Waiting until junior or senior year to consider this may make it impossible. Not all of your course requirements will be offered abroad, so you'll have to plan your four-year curriculum path accordingly. Meet with your adviser and/or the study-abroad office, and they'll help you plan it out and tell you if and how it will affect your graduation date.

If you can't do a whole semester due to fulfilling your graduation requirements or because it's just way too long for you to be gone, study abroad over a summer or winter break.

Another excuse for not studying abroad is the cost. The truth is that it's not much more expensive than another semester on campus. Look into study-abroad scholarships and how your financial aid may be able to contribute. Compare the cost of a study-abroad semester now to going on a four-month vacation later in life. You're saving money in the long run and hammering out credits for graduation in the process.

Even if you're a homebody and the thought of going abroad scares the shit out of you, do it. My friend Lauren from the last chapter is very much this type of person, but she went abroad for a month-long course and absolutely loved it.

It may seem like a full semester is a long time to be abroad, but you're not committing your whole life. You're committing four months that have the potential to change your whole life. Don't say no because you don't want to miss out on things at school. You have eight semesters; take one to do something amazing.

## FINAL THOUGHTS

Usually people feel held back by something when it comes to studying abroad: money, women, fear, or other obligations.
Don't be held back. Go abroad.

# 7.4 NETWORKING

In our minds, this is the single most important aspect of college to take advantage of. You have the opportunity to meet hundreds of people who may have future opportunities to offer you: professors, coaches, advisers, employers, and friends. Each of those people knows a hundred more. If you voice your intentions to your people, whether they involve employment opportunities, academic needs, or passions, someone eventually will have an opportunity for you.

The relationships you cultivate are much more important than a few As on your transcript. *At the end of the day, no one really cares about your GPA.* No one wants to work with someone who's slightly smarter than the next guy but also a total dick.

*Unless you plan to apply to grad school, medical school, law school, etc.*

If you suck at talking to people, read Dale Carnegie's *How to Win Friends & Influence People*. The title sounds manipulative, but this book is a great resource for how to become a better people person. Carnegie takes a pragmatic approach to improving personal relationships, equipping the reader with tools for everyday conversations.

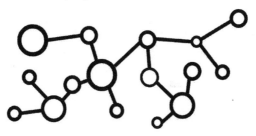

## FINAL THOUGHTS

I am not especially smart or a naturally great leader. I credit my successes in school, leadership roles, and employment opportunities simply to being kind and building relationships with people.

# FIN

I hope you and your offspring are able to benefit from our experiences, mistakes, and lessons learned during our collegiate campaign.

I'm proud of you. If anything, you've proven to yourself that you can read a full book cover to cover. I'd suggest you continue doing so, furthering your education in preparation for life. If you're need some ideas for additional reading, see the list in the appendix, which includes titles I've referenced throughout the book plus a few more keepers.

Spread the knowledge. Knowing you shared this with your roommates and friends would make me warm inside. Keep 'er movin'.

-Andrew

# CHEAT SHEET

## KILL IT IN SCHOOL

Use Ratemyprofessors.com to your benefit.
Manage your time. Grind during the day; have fun later.
Be engaged in class and in the library. Put your phone away.

## SAVE MONEY

Do not buy textbooks unless you have to.
Find a job that has more to offer you (financially or otherwise) than minimum wage.
Take classes elsewhere and transfer your credits. Apply for scholarships every year.

## HAVE FUN

Be uncomfortable. Introduce yourself to everyone. Make tons of new friends.
Close the yearbook (for the most part).
Be an individual.
Drink smarter, not harder.
Take care of your mind and body.
Grow some balls when it comes to women.
Chivalry is not dead.

## HAVE A FUTURE

Have your résumé and cover letter at the ready.
Use your summers. Intern as early as possible.
Study abroad.
Network, network, network.

# FURTHER EDUCATION

*The Happiness Hypothesis,* by Jonathan Haidt

*How to Win Friends & Influence People,* by Dale Carnegie

*The Evolution of Desire: Strategies of Human Mating,* by David M. Buss

*You Are a Badass: How to Stop Doubting Your Greatness and Start Living an Awesome Life,* by Jen Sincero

*The 4-Hour Body,* by Tim Ferris

*In Defense of Food,* by Michael Pollan

*The Servant: A Simple Story about the True Essence of Leadership,* by James C. Hunter

"Tips for College Freshmen," by Jimmy Tatro on YouTube

# GOLD-STAR SPONSORS

Thank you for your support!

| | |
|---|---|
| Kristine Sorenson | Rick, Isa, and Alexa Bohon |
| Cody Kaye | Nick & Mel Cocalis |
| Chris, Cindy, Cam & Cage Cocalis | Drew Harrison |
| Geoff McQuillan | Jim Ferry |
| The Grammy | Andrew Broman |
| Jamey & Amy Sotis | Ann Merfeld |
| Paul Vijums | Mary Beth Arnold |
| Heidi & Mark Lucarelli | JB Stender |
| Dennis Fortier | John Michael Coon |
| Maia Sotis | Andrew Werlin |
| Patti Sotis | Peter Schubloom |
| Lisa Sotis | Karin Thysse |
| Debra McNeil | Todd & Mary Argall |
| Jesse O'Brien | Dan Gill |

# GOOD LUCK!

Pictured: Illustrator and author, looking their best.

71915952R00046

Made in the USA
Middletown, DE
01 May 2018